D0021196

Paul Gayler is executive chef at The Lanesborough in London, one of the most fabulous destination hotels in the world. He has worked in some of London's most prestigious restaurants, including The Dorchester and Inigo Jones. Paul has appeared on BBC2's *Saturday Kitchen* and Radio 4's *VegTalk*, as well as being a judge on ITV's *Chef of the Year*. His previous books for Kyle Cathie have been translated into 10 languages and sold 500,000 copies worldwide.

Paul Gayler's **little book of**

salads

Paul Gayler's **little book of**

salads

stunning, healthy, ready in minutes

Kyle Cathie Limited

For the New Age foodies who demand quality, taste and innovation.

First published in Great Britain in 2009 by
Kyle Cathie Limited
122 Arlington Road
London NW1 7HP
www.kylecathie.com

ISBN 978 1 85626 840 0

Text © 2009 Paul Gayler

All rights reserved. No reproduction, copy or transmission of this publication may be made without written permission. No paragraph of this publication may be reproduced, copied or transmitted save with written permission or in accordance with the provisions of the Copyright Act 1956 (as amended). Any person who does any unauthorised act in relation to this publication may be liable to criminal prosecution and civil claims for damages.

Edited by Barbara Bonser
Designed by Mark Jonathan Latter @ Pink Stripe Design
New photography by Will Heap
Styling for new photography by Sheiko and Silvana Franco
Other photographs by Gus Filgate, Lisa Linder, Steve Lee and Georgia Glynn Smith

Paul Gayler is hereby identified as the author of this work in accordance with Section 77 of the Copyright, Designs and Patents Act 1988.

A Cataloguing in Publication record for this title is available from the British Library.

contents

introduction

As lighter and healthier eating habits have become the norm over recent years, salads are playing an increasingly important role in meal planning. Salads make light and stimulating appetisers, as well as satisfying main meals. A good salad can consist of nothing more than a few sweet inner salad leaves, tossed lightly in a mustard and vinegar dressing, while others can be beautifully composed and include a myriad of ingredients served raw, cooked and served cold, or even warm.

The most important ingredients are freshness and quality. No amount of dressing, scattering of herbs, or creative seasoning will disguise the disappointing texture and flavour of limp and wilted leaves, or overly mature ingredients.

I have included designer-style salads for the beginner as well as the experienced cook, all vibrant, nutritious and varied. The salads use ingredients from most food categories – vegetables, fish, seafood, meat, cereals, and grains – and many are inspired by foreign cuisine. My aim has been to excite you with new tastes and combinations which I hope will act as an inspirational starting point for your very own salad creations.

All recipes serve four people.

salad tips

• Coat your salad with its dressing at the last possible minute.

• Treat delicate salad leaves gently, or you will bruise them. Tear leaves rather than cutting them, because cut edges tend to turn brown.

• Ensure leaves are dried thoroughly with a clean tea towel, or in a salad spinner.

• Dunk tightly packed leaves, such as radicchio and cos, briefly in lightly salted water. Never leave them to soak.

• Always have an eye for colour, not necessarily contrast. Keep it fresh-looking and elegant.

• Think about the variations of texture and ensure that they are balanced, for example, crisp, crunchy or soft.

• Always use the best quality oils and vinegar you can find. Nut oils such as hazelnut and walnut should always be refrigerated because they are unstable and easily turn rancid.

dressings

A basic vinaigrette dressing is three parts oil, to one part vinegar or lemon juice, but some cooks prefer a little more oil to tone down the acidity. A little Dijon mustard is often added and salt and pepper to taste.

Olive oil is the traditional choice, but I often choose a mild variety or mix it with a sunflower, grape seed or rapeseed oil. Certain dressings may require stronger flavoured oil such as walnut or hazelnut, a blander oil such as ground nut is an alternative.

Numerous vinegars are available, all differing widely in flavour, strength and character. Red and white wine, sherry and sweet balsamic are the most popular. Greens that have a strong leaf structure and taste are best partnered with stronger vinegars such as red wine and sherry. Chicories, which include curly endive and radicchio, may need a little added balsamic sweetness.

Once you have chosen your oil and vinegar, blend them together with mustard, cream, or a few drops of water to help bring it all together.

Other dressings are based on mayonnaise, sour cream or yogurt. I often blend them with goat's or blue cheese, fresh herbs, watercress or roasted red peppers. Asian-style dressings with lime juice, soy and *nam pla* (Thai fish sauce), perfectly complement noodle salads.

Each salad in this book has its own dressing recipe. I hope you will adapt these to suit your own individual taste.

finishing touches

• Brush diced bread with olive oil and toast until golden to make croûtons.
• Lightly toast or caramelise walnuts, hazelnuts, pine nuts and cashews in a little sugar.
• Lightly toast sunflower or pumpkin seeds, taking care not to burn them.
• Crumble Mexican corn tortillas or Indian poppadums.

mediterranean

Salade monégasque is similar to salade niçoise and is prepared daily in cafés and brasseries all over France. It is normally served on its own but I prefer it with char-grilled fish. Mackerel would work just as well as sardines.

salade monégasque

with char-grilled sardines

225g small new potatoes
150g French beans
4 anchovy fillets, cut into strips
2 teaspoons superfine capers,
  rinsed and drained
4 radishes, thinly shaved
12 black olives, pitted
1 celery stick, thinly sliced
12 cherry tomatoes, halved
2 hard-boiled eggs, cut into quarters
salt and freshly ground black pepper
4 x 225g fresh sardines, filleted

for the dressing
2 tablespoons good quality white
  wine vinegar
2 garlic cloves, crushed
1 teaspoon Dijon mustard
salt
6 tablespoons olive oil,
  plus extra for grilling

Cook the unpeeled potatoes and the French beans in separate pans of boiling salted water until just tender, then drain well.

For the dressing, whisk the vinegar, garlic, mustard and a little salt together in a large bowl, then whisk in the oil. Add the potatoes and beans to the bowl, then add all the remaining ingredients except the sardines. Toss gently and season with salt and pepper.

Heat a ridged grill pan and brush with a little oil. Place the sardine fillets on the grill and cook for 2–3 minutes on each side, until golden. Arrange the salad on serving plates, top with the chargrilled sardines and drizzle over a little of the dressing left in the bowl.

Flatbread is available from good Italian delicatessens; it is sometimes called *carta musica* or music sheets, as it is very thin. There are also many varieties of Middle Eastern-style flatbread which can be used.

chickpea salad

with feta-baked flatbread

4 sheets Sardinian flatbread,
  broken into large pieces
50g feta cheese, crumbled
400g tinned chickpeas,
  drained and rinsed
200g cherry tomatoes
20 black olives, pitted
75g flat parsley leaves
1 tablespoon pine kernels, toasted
2 bunches watercress

for the dressing
1 tablespoon *tahini* (sesame seed paste)
1 garlic clove, crushed
100ml water
65ml low-fat
  natural yogurt
juice of ½ lemon
freshly ground black pepper

Preheat the oven to 200°C/400°F/gas mark 6.

Lay the flatbread on a large baking sheet, sprinkle over the crumbled feta and bake for 2–3 minutes until the cheese begins to melt.

In a bowl, whisk all the ingredients for the dressing together and season with black pepper to taste.

Place the chickpeas, tomatoes, olives, parsley, pine kernels and watercress in another bowl, pour over the dressing and toss lightly together.

Layer the salad with the flatbread and serve.

A simple but tasty salad, full of the robust flavours of Provence. Don't worry if you haven't got a pestle and mortar for the dressing; use a small blender instead.

grilled potato
& fennel niçoise

3 fennel bulbs
350g large new potatoes
4 tablespoons olive oil
salt and freshly ground
  black pepper

for the dressing
1 garlic clove, chopped
8 basil leaves
salt
2 red peppers, roasted,
  skinned, deseeded and
  finely chopped
10 black olives, pitted
  and finely chopped
2 shallots, finely chopped
4 anchovy fillets,
  finely chopped
5 tablespoons olive oil
juice of ½ lemon

Remove any fronds from the fennel and set aside. Peel the fennel with a potato peeler to remove the fibrous outer layer. Cut each bulb in half lengthways, then cut each half into eight thin wedges. Trim off a little of the root from each piece but be careful to leave the layers attached at the root end.

Bring 2 pans of water to the boil. Add the fennel to one and the new potatoes to the other. Cook the fennel for 3–4 minutes, then drain in a colander. Let the new potatoes cook on until they are just tender when pierced with a knife. Drain in a colander and cool slightly before cutting them in half lengthways. Heat a ridged grill pan, toss the fennel wedges and potatoes in the olive oil and season with salt and pepper. Cook on the grill, turning them often, until golden and tender.

Meanwhile, prepare the dressing. Place the garlic, basil and a good pinch of salt in a mortar and crush to a paste. Stir in the remaining ingredients and season to taste.

Put the grilled potatoes and fennel in a bowl, pour over the dressing and garnish with any reserved fennel fronds.

In this chilli-pickled salad the oranges are marinated in vinegar and sugar overnight to give a refreshing sweet and sour flavour. Always try to obtain genuine Greek feta, which is generally made of 30 per cent goat's milk and 70 per cent sheep's milk.

tangy orange, feta & olive salad

4 oranges, preferably navel
90ml white wine vinegar
3 tablespoons castor sugar
1 red chilli, thinly sliced into rings
90ml olive oil
salt and freshly ground black pepper
2 tablespoons black olives
175g feta, cut into 1cm cubes
1 tablespoon chopped fresh oregano
   or parsley
1 teaspoon cracked black pepper
   (see PG TIPS)
baby spinach and rocket leaves,
   to garnish (optional)

Peel the oranges, removing all the white pith, and cut into slices 5mm thick. Remove pips and put the orange slices in a shallow dish. Boil the vinegar and sugar together for 2–3 minutes, add the chilli and then pour on to the orange slices. Cover and leave overnight.

Drain off the juices from the pickled oranges into a bowl. Whisk in the olive oil and season with salt and pepper. Arrange the oranges in a serving bowl. Stir the olives, feta and oregano or parsley into the dressing and sprinkle it over the oranges. Sprinkle with coarsely cracked black pepper. Scatter over the spinach and rocket leaves, if using, and serve.

PG TIPS
To make cracked black pepper, put some peppercorns in a pestle and mortar and pound to break roughly.

pickled blue cheese salad

with *kadaifi* fritters

for the *kadaifi* fritters
1 Granny Smith apple, cored
  and finely diced
juice of ½ lemon
125g creamy blue cheese, crumbled
½ teaspoon Dijon mustard
pinch of paprika
175g fresh white breadcrumbs
1 free-range egg yolk
little flour
100g *kadaifi* pastry (shredded filo
  pastry available from Middle
  Eastern or Greek stores)
40g unsalted butter, melted
vegetable oil for deep-frying
salt, freshly ground black pepper
ground nutmeg

for the pickled blue cheese salad
2 tablespoons castor sugar
4 tablespoons red wine vinegar
1 carrot, peeled
75g celeriac, peeled
1 red onion, peeled and thinly sliced
75g baby spinach leaves
30g fresh flat leaf parsley leaves
50g rocket leaves
75g blue cheese, frozen for
  10 minutes and shaved

Coat the diced apple with the lemon juice and toss
together for 1 minute. Place the crumbled cheese in a
bowl and add the apple, mustard, paprika, breadcrumbs
and finally the egg yolk. Season and bring the mixture
together to a thick paste that holds its shape. Refrigerate
for 2 hours, then remove and shape into eight small
patties. Dust with a little flour.

Carefully unwrap the *kadaifi* pastry and spread it out on
to a work surface. Liberally brush the pastry strands with
melted butter, then wrap the patties in it ensuring the
pastry completely covers them. Set aside.

For the salad, heat the sugar and vinegar in a pan and
boil for 1 minute. Using a kitchen mandolin or sharp
knife, shred the carrot and celeriac into a bowl and add
the thinly sliced onion. Pour over the hot vinegar and
leave to cool. When cold, add the spinach, parsley and
rocket and toss well together. Finally add half the cheese.

Fry the *kadaifi* fritters for about 3–4 minutes until golden
and crispy, remove and drain on kitchen paper. Pile the
salad high on 4 plates, place 2 fritters per person on top
of each salad and sprinkle over the remaining shaved
cheese. Alternatively serve the salad separately.

Morocco boasts one of the most exciting cuisines in the world, a subtle blend of African and European influences. This salad is adapted from one prepared for me by a street vendor at the world-renowned Djema'a al Fna square in Marrakech.

Moroccan sweet potato & coriander salad

150ml good quality olive oil
2 onions, thinly sliced
1cm piece of fresh root ginger, finely chopped
2 red chillies, deseeded and thinly sliced
600g small, white-fleshed sweet potatoes, peeled and cut into slices 3mm thick
pinch of saffron strands
½ teaspoon cumin seeds, toasted briefly in a dry frying pan
juice of 1 lemon
½ teaspoon smoked paprika
3 tablespoons chopped coriander
1 tablespoon chopped mint
1 tablespoon finely chopped preserved lemon
salt and freshly ground black pepper

Heat 100ml olive oil in a large pan, add the onions, ginger and chillies and sauté until tender but not coloured. Add the sweet potatoes, saffron, cumin seeds, lemon juice and smoked paprika, then pour in enough water just to cover.

Cover the pan with a lid, reduce the heat and cook for 10–12 minutes, until the potatoes are just tender. Stir in the coriander, mint and preserved lemon, then pour over the remaining oil and adjust the seasoning. Transfer to a bowl and leave to cool before serving.

PG TIPS
Preserved salted lemons are one of the definitive flavours of Moroccan cooking. You can buy them from delicatessens and large supermarkets.

I love the combination of salty feta cheese with sweet beetroot and apricot, pepped up by a little chilli. A colourful salad with heavenly flavours.

roasted beetroot, feta & apricot salad

900g baby beetroot
3 tablespoons groundnut oil
450g fresh apricots
100g feta cheese,
  crumbled
2 tablespoons walnuts

for the vinaigrette
2 teaspoons sherry vinegar
2 teaspoons honey
1 serrano chilli, thinly sliced
3 tablespoons olive oil
3 tablespoons groundnut oil
salt and freshly ground
  black pepper

Preheat the oven to 180°C/350°F/gas mark 4. Trim the leafy tops off the beetroot and scrub the bulbs well. Place in a baking tin, drizzle over the groundnut oil, cover the tin with foil and bake for 1–1½ hours, until tender. Remove from the oven and leave to cool, then peel carefully or rub off the skins. Place in a bowl.

Blanch the apricots in boiling water for 1 minute to loosen the skin, plunge into iced water, then peel them. Cut in half, remove the stones and place the apricots in a bowl.

To make the vinaigrette, mix together the vinegar, honey and chilli, whisk in both the oils and season with salt and pepper.

Dress the beetroot and the apricots with the vinaigrette (keeping them separate, otherwise the beetroot will 'bleed' into the apricots) and leave for 20 minutes to marinate. Arrange on a serving plate, sprinkle over the crumbled feta cheese and the walnuts and serve at room temperature.

Ajo-blanco, a peppery almond and garlic dressing from Spain, perfectly complements the flavour of artichokes.

Jerusalem artichoke salad

with beans, fennel and *ajo-blanco*

for the green peppercorn *ajo-blanco*
50g whole blanched almonds
25g pine nuts
2 garlic cloves, crushed
50g fresh white breadcrumbs
100ml iced water
4 tablespoons extra virgin olive oil
2 tablespoons sherry vinegar
2 free-range egg yolks
salt
4 tablespoons double cream
1 teaspoon green peppercorns,
   rinsed and drained

for the salad
16 Jerusalem artichokes
200g French beans, topped
   and tailed
1 large head of fennel, fronds
   removed
splash of sherry vinegar
2 tablespoons extra virgin olive oil
1 large shallot, thinly sliced
50g flaked almonds, toasted
salt and freshly ground black pepper

For the *ajo-blanco*, place the almonds, pine nuts and garlic in a food processor and blend as fine as possible. Do not over-process. Add the breadcrumbs and a quarter of the iced water and blend again to a fine purée. With the motor running, gently pour in a thin stream of the oil and half the vinegar. When smooth, add the egg yolks and blitz again. Strain into a bowl, add salt and the remaining water and vinegar. Stir in the cream, add the peppercorns and refrigerate. It should be the consistency of single cream – if it's too thick add a little more water.

For the salad, wash and peel the artichokes, cutting off the knobbly bits. Cook them in lightly simmering salted water for 12–15 minutes. Drain and then slice them into 5cm thick pieces. Keep warm. At the same time, cook the French beans for 4–5 minutes until just tender. Drain well and add to the artichokes.

Using a kitchen mandolin, thinly shave the fennel on to the artichokes and beans, add a splash of vinegar, the olive oil and shallot slices and season to taste. Add the dressing, toss carefully together and adjust seasoning. Garnish with the toasted almonds.

exotic

smoked paprika feta salad

with sweet lemon dressing

for the cigarillos
2 sheets filo pastry
200g ready-to-eat dates,
  chopped finely
vegetable oil for deep-frying

for the salad
2 tablespoons olive oil
4 red peppers, halved and deseeded
240g feta cheese, cut into large dice
1 teaspoon smoked paprika
12 black olives
1 red onion, thinly sliced
2 tablespoons flaked almonds,
  toasted

for the dressing
2 lemons, halved
3 tablespoons argan oil
  (or olive oil)
pinch of good cinnamon
½ garlic clove, crushed
pinch of sumac (optional)
30g chopped fresh mint
1 teaspoon castor sugar
salt and freshly ground
  black pepper

Lay a sheet of filo pastry on a work surface and cut into four equal rectangles. Place a spoonful of the dates at the short end of each filo rectangle. Tightly roll up the pastry, tucking the sides in as you near the end. Seal the last 5cm of the cigarillo with a little cold water. Set aside. Repeat.

Heat a ridged grill pan until very hot, brush with the olive oil. Cut each pepper half into three strips lengthways. Place on the grill and cook until tender and slightly charred, turning them regularly. Remove and peel off their skin. Leave to cool, then transfer to a bowl.

For the dressing, grill the lemon halves for 2–3 minutes until slightly cooked and lightly charred. Remove and cool slightly, then squeeze the juice into a bowl and add the remaining ingredients; season to taste.

Dust the feta pieces lightly with smoked paprika. Add the olives, onion and almonds to the pepper, pour over a little of the lemon dressing and season to taste. Place the salad on a serving plate, top with the paprika-dusted feta and drizzle over the remaining dressing.

Heat the vegetable oil to 180°C/350°F, drop the date cigarillos into the hot oil and cook for 1 minute until golden and crispy. Remove and drain on kitchen paper.

Fish and meat in fragrant Asian dressings really hit the spot. Here is my version, using Vietnamese mint as a prime ingredient. I find it best served at room temperature.

minted chicken & aubergine salad

sesame oil
4 skinless, boneless chicken breasts
1 aubergine, cut into 1 cm slices
2 tablespoons brown sugar
1 tablespoon *nam pla*
  (Thai fish sauce; see PG TIPS, p.37)
1 garlic clove, crushed
2 green chillies, thinly sliced
juice of 4 limes
1 lemongrass stalk, outer layers
  removed, tender inner core very
  finely chopped
1 onion, thinly sliced
2 shallots, chopped
salt and freshly ground black pepper
50g Vietnamese mint leaves
4 tablespoons roasted peanuts,
  chopped

Heat a ridged grill pan, brush it with a little sesame oil, then season the chicken breasts and place on the grill. Cook for 5–6 minutes on each side, until lightly charred and cooked through. Brush the aubergine slices with sesame oil, place on the grill and cook until lightly charred, turning them regularly and brushing with a little more oil if necessary.

Meanwhile, place the sugar in a bowl, add the fish sauce, garlic, chillies and lime juice and mix well. Stir in the lemongrass, onion and shallots.

Remove the chicken and aubergine from the grill and leave to cool, then shred the chicken and cut the aubergine into small dice. Add to the bowl, season, toss well, cover with clingfilm and leave to marinate at room temperature for 1 hour.

Add the mint leaves and serve in a deep bowl, sprinkled with the peanuts.

A salad I have prepared for numerous dinner parties, with great success. Other shellfish could be substituted if preferred.

spiced prawn salad

(pla talay)

2 tablespoons lime juice
1 tablespoon *nam pla* (Thai fish sauce)
1 teaspoon sesame oil
2 tablespoons soy sauce
1 small red chilli, deseeded and finely chopped
½ garlic clove, crushed
1 teaspoon castor sugar
1 avocado
400g fresh or frozen large tiger prawns, cooked
2 lemongrass sticks, very finely shredded
2 shallots, thinly sliced
2 tablespoon finely shredded mint leaves
4 spring onions, halved and finely shredded lengthways
1 green papaya, peeled and finely shredded (optional)
100g watercress

In a bowl, mix together the lime juice, fish sauce, sesame oil and soy sauce, then add the chopped chilli. Add the garlic and sugar and mix well together.

Cut the avocado in half lengthways, remove the stone and halve again. Carefully peel off the outer skin and cut the flesh into long, thin slices. Add the prawns and avocado to the bowl.

Add the remaining ingredients and carefully toss the lot together. Dress on individual plates and serve immediately.

PG TIPS

Fish sauce is a condiment that is derived from fish that has been allowed to ferment. It is a staple ingredient in Thai, Vietnamese and other South-east Asian cuisines. It is added to the cooking process or in a mixed form with other ingredients as a dipping condiment.

Dishes using fish sauce rarely have added salt in them as the sauce itself is salty in flavour.

This Japanese-inspired salad uses *wasabi tobiko*, the orangey-red roe of a type of flying fish. It is available in oriental shops.

smoked salmon salad

with simple crab sushi

150g short grain rice, rinsed
350ml water
1 tablespoon rice vinegar
2 teaspoons sugar
125g fresh white crabmeat
100g mixed bitter salad leaves,
    such as peashoots, dandelion,
    mizuna and frisée, torn into
    small pieces
4 red radishes, thinly sliced
1 tablespoon pickled pink ginger,
    shredded
15g *hijiki* seaweed
225g thinly sliced smoked salmon
1 tablespoon *wasabi tobiko* or other
    fish roe

for the dressing
½ teaspoon *sansho* (Japanese pepper)
2 tablespoons red wine vinegar
2 tablespoons light soy sauce
4 tablespoons sesame oil
4 tablespoons vegetable oil
juice of ½ lemon
2 teaspoons Asian sweet chilli sauce

Place the rice in saucepan, pour over 350ml water and quickly bring to the boil. Reduce the heat, cover and simmer until all the liquid has been absorbed. Remove from the heat and set aside for 5 minutes.

In a small pan, gently heat the vinegar and sugar. Spread the cooked rice out on a large flat tray, then sprinkle over the vinegar and sugar. Gently mix it with the rice and leave to cool.

Mix the crabmeat with the salad leaves, radishes, ginger and seaweed, then toss with the cooled sushi rice.

Place 4 lightly oiled ring moulds or pastry cutters about 7.5cm in diameter on a tray, and line the inner edges with bands of smoked salmon. Fill the centres with the sushi salad, taking it right to the top. Mix together all the ingredients for the dressing.

Place one ring on each serving plate and carefully remove the ring. Top each with a little fish roe, if using and pour a little of the dressing around.

This salad of crunchy vegetables and beansprouts in a spicy sweet peanut dressing comes from Indonesia.

gado gado

for the peanut sauce
6 tablespoons sesame oil
1 red Thai chilli, deseeded
  and finely chopped
100g smooth peanut butter
6 tablespoons vegetable stock
  or water
2 tablespoons mango chutney
5 tablespoons coconut milk
1 garlic clove, crushed
1 tablespoon soy sauce
2 teaspoons brown sugar
salt and freshly ground black pepper
juice of 1 lemon

1 waxy potato
2 carrots, cut into matchsticks
100g French beans
75g cucumber,
  cut into matchsticks
50g beansprouts
½ Chinese cabbage, leaves
  separated
8 quail's eggs, hard-boiled,
  shelled and halved

For the sauce, heat 5 tablespoons of the sesame oil in a small saucepan and fry the chilli in it until soft. In another pan, heat the peanut butter, then add the stock or water, mango chutney and coconut milk and boil for 2 minutes. Add the chilli and its oil and remove from the heat, then add the garlic, soy sauce, remaining sesame oil and the sugar. Season to taste and add the lemon juice; the sauce may separate slightly. Keep warm.

Boil the potato until tender, drain, then peel while it is still hot. Slice and keep warm. Cook the carrots and beans separately in boiling salted water, retaining their crispness. Drain them and add to the potatoes with the cucumber and beansprouts.

To serve, season the warm vegetables. Arrange the Chinese cabbage leaves on serving plates and top with the warm vegetables and quail's eggs. Coat lightly with the sauce and serve.

PG TIPS
This is also very good with the addition of some sliced tofu, fried in a little vegetable oil until golden brown.

This dish is usually made with plain roast chicken, but smoked chicken makes a nice alternative. *Murgh* means chicken and *chat* means to savour, and this is indeed a tempting salad, ideal for the summer months.

spiced chicken & mango salad

(murgh chat)

juice of 2 limes
juice of ½ lemon
1 garlic clove, crushed
2 tablespoons maple syrup
1 cooked smoked chicken,
  skin removed and meat shredded
2 ripe plum tomatoes, skinned,
  deseeded and chopped
1 green chilli, deseeded
  and very finely chopped
½ cucumber, deseeded and chopped
2 red onions, finely sliced
1 green pepper, deseeded
  and chopped
1 teaspoon cumin seeds,
  lightly toasted
2 tablespoons roughly chopped
  coriander leaves
1 tablespoon roughly chopped mint
1 mango, peeled and cut into wedges
freshly ground black pepper

In a bowl whisk the juice of the limes and lemon with the garlic and maple syrup. Add the remaining ingredients and toss well together.

Marinate for 30 minutes before serving to allow the flavours to meld.

PG TIPS

I would suggest using Indian Alphonso mangoes for this salad. They are generally more expensive than other mangoes, but their perfume-like fragrance and sweet flavour really makes the salad. They have a short season, April to May, and a short shelf life. It is best to seek them out in ethnic stores and food markets.

What I like about this salad is the combination of chewy fish and tangy, lightly char-grilled fruit. It makes a wonderful starter for a summer dinner.

grilled squid & melon salad

with hot and sour kaffir dressing

225g cleaned squid
¼ honeydew melon, peeled
 and cut into thin wedges
a slice of watermelon,
 peeled and cut into thin wedges
1 tablespoon roughly chopped
 mint leaves
1 tablespoon roughly chopped
 coriander leaves

for the marinade
100ml olive oil
¼ teaspoon chilli powder
1 garlic clove
juice of 1 lime
2 tablespoons sugar

for the dressing
3 tablespoons *nam pla*
 (Thai fish sauce)
2 tablespoons lime juice
1 garlic clove, crushed
1 red and 1 green chilli,
 deseeded and finely chopped
1 teaspoon brown sugar
4 kaffir lime leaves, finely shredded
 (see PG TIPS, p.48)

Slit the squid bodies open, cut them into large rectangles and then score in a diamond pattern on the inner side with a sharp knife (this makes them curl up attractively when cooked). Leave the tentacles in large pieces.

Mix all the marinade ingredients together in a large bowl, add the squid and melon and leave to marinate at room temperature for 2–3 hours.

Heat the grill to its highest setting. Remove the squid and melon from the marinade, place on the grill pan and grill for 4–5 minutes. Transfer to a bowl and sprinkle over the mint and coriander leaves.

Put all the ingredients for the dressing into a pan and heat gently. Pour the dressing over the squid and melon. Leave to cool to room temperature before serving.

I love warm salads, especially those with an oriental flavour. Chicken can be used instead of duck, if preferred. *Ketjap manis* is Indonesian soy sauce, made from black soya beans.

wok-seared duck salad

with lemongrass and ginger dressing

for the dressing
5cm piece of fresh root ginger
100ml orange juice
2 tablespoons balsamic vinegar
2 tablespoons *ketjap manis*
  (Indonesian soy sauce) or soy sauce
2 lemongrass sticks, finely chopped
1 garlic clove, crushed
1 tablespoon sweet chilli sauce

1 teaspoon unsaturated oil
4 x 150g duck breasts, skin removed
1 tablespoon brown sugar
4 tablespoons orange juice
2 tablespoons *ketjap manis*
  (Indonesian soy sauce) or soy sauce
2½cm piece of fresh root ginger, peeled
1 garlic clove
12 broccoli florets
150g mixed salad leaves
1 carrot, finely shredded
75g beansprouts
freshly ground black pepper
4 tablespoons flaked almonds, toasted

To make the dressing, use a fine grater to grate the ginger into a bowl, then squeeze or strain through muslin so you are left with the juice only. Add the remaining ingredients and season to taste. Set aside.

Heat the oil in a wok, add the duck breasts and seal all over. Then add the sugar, orange juice, soy sauce, ginger and garlic and cook for 10–12 minutes, basting regularly until the duck is cooked and glazed all over. Remove and keep warm.

Cook the broccoli in boiling water. Place the salad leaves, broccoli, carrot and beansprouts in a bowl, add a little dressing and toss well. Season with black pepper to taste.

Cut the duck into thin slices, top with salad, pour over a little dressing and serve, scattered with the toasted almonds.

This refreshing hot, sweet and sour fruit salad is from Bali, where it is a popular snack. It makes a wonderful starter or an addition to any buffet. Topped with ice cream, it can also be served as an intriguing dessert.

rujak

50g palm sugar
2 tablespoons tamarind paste
100ml water
pinch of salt
3 red Thai chillies,
   deseeded and finely chopped
salt
1 small pineapple, peeled, cored
   and cut into small wedges
1 green mango, peeled, stoned
   and sliced
1 pink grapefruit, peeled and
   cut into segments
1 green apple, peeled, cored
   and cut into 1cm dice
1 papaya, peeled, deseeded
   and cut into wedges

Put the palm sugar and tamarind paste in a small pan with the water and a pinch of salt. Boil for 2 minutes, then add the chillies and leave to infuse for a few minutes.

Place all the chopped fruit in a serving bowl and pour over the hot syrup mixture. Mix in gently and well, then leave to cool to room temperature before serving.

PG TIPS
Tamarind paste is available in speciality stores in paste or pod form. It has a tart yet sweet flavour and is used in more sauces than you would think: Worcester Sauce or HP sauce, for example.

This Indian salad, served at room temperature, is fantastic with a tart apple and grape chutney. It also makes a nice addition to an Asian meal.

aloo chat

100g ghee or clarified butter
1 small onion, finely chopped
450g small waxy potatoes, peeled
  and cut lengthways in half
1 small red chilli, deseeded and
  thinly sliced
1 teaspoon ground turmeric
2 teaspoons ground coriander
1 teaspoon cumin seeds, toasted
  briefly in a dry frying pan
salt
150ml water
flesh from ½ small coconut, cut
  into shavings (see PG TIPS)
fresh coriander leaves, to garnish

Heat the ghee or clarified butter in a frying pan, add the onion and cook over a low heat until translucent. Add the potatoes, chilli, turmeric, ground coriander, cumin seeds and a little salt and fry for 10–15 minutes, until the potatoes are lightly browned.

Add the water and bring to the boil. Reduce the heat to a simmer and cook gently until all the liquid has been absorbed and the potatoes are tender. Leave to cool, then arrange in a serving dish. Scatter over the coconut shavings and coriander leaves before serving.

PG TIPS
To shave fresh coconut, cut a coconut in half with a saw and pour off the liquid. Knock the base of the coconut hard with a rolling pin to loosen the flesh, then run a knife around the edge – the flesh should come away in one piece. Cut into shavings with a potato peeler or a mandolin.

The contrasting colours and textures of mussels, prawns and squid combine perfectly with a sharp spicy dressing to make this stunning salad.

spicy mixed seafood salad

1kg mussels
2 tablespoons groundnut oil
450g large raw prawns,
   peeled and deveined
450g small squid,
   cut into small sections

for the dressing
2 garlic cloves, crushed
2 tablespoons finely
   chopped coriander
2.5cm piece of fresh root
   ginger, finely chopped
4 kaffir lime leaves, finely shredded
300ml unsweetened coconut cream
2 tablespoons Asian sweet
   chilli sauce
juice and zest of 1 lime
25g coriander leaves
12 small mint leaves

Scrub the mussels under cold running water, removing the beards and discarding any open mussels that don't close when tapped on a work surface. Place the mussels in a steamer and steam over a high heat until opened. Remove from the steamer and discard the shells.

Heat the oil in a frying pan, add the prawns and squid and fry over a high heat for 1–2 minutes only. Add the shelled mussels and place in a bowl.

Mix together all the ingredients for the dressing and pour it over the seafood. Allow to cool and serve at room temperature.

PG TIPS
Kaffir lime leaves are the dark green fragrant leaves of the kaffir lime used in South-east Asian countries. They add an indispensable perfume unlike any other citrus fruit to many dishes including soups, salads and curries. They tend to be frozen when transported in from Thailand due to import restrictions.

A healthy and beautifully flavoured dish. Green papaya salad (*som tam*) is a staple dish from north-east Thailand, prepared daily by roadside traders.

papaya salad

with char-grilled tuna

650g small tuna fillet, trimmed
2 tablespoons tamarind paste
2 tablespoons brown sugar
2 red chillies, deseeded
  and finely chopped
1 tablespoon *nam pla*
  (Thai fish sauce)
salt and freshly ground black pepper
a little oil for grilling
1 lime, cut into wedges, to garnish

for the green papaya salad
1 garlic clove, chopped
2 red chillies, deseeded and chopped
1 teaspoon brown sugar
2 green papayas, peeled,
  deseeded and shredded
juice of 2 limes
2 tablespoons *nam pla*
  (Thai fish sauce)
100g French beans, cooked
2 tablespoons roasted peanuts
10 red cherry tomatoes, halved
10 yellow cherry tomatoes, halved

Cut the tuna into 4 steaks across the fillet. In a bowl, combine the tamarind paste with the sugar, chillies, fish sauce and some salt and pepper. Pour this mixture over the tuna and set aside for 1 hour to allow the flavours to meld.

For the salad, roughly crush the garlic, chillies, sugar and a quarter of the shredded papaya in a mortar. Transfer to a bowl, add the lime juice and fish sauce and stir well. Add all the remaining ingredients, including the rest of the papaya, toss well and season to taste.

Heat a ridged grill pan until very hot and brush with a little oil. Season the tuna steaks again with salt and pepper and char-grill for 2 minutes on each side, keeping them rare. Remove from the grill and cut each steak into 4 slices.

Arrange a pile of salad on each serving plate, top with the seared tuna. Garnish with the lime wedges and serve.

Indian bread salad

with grilled paneer cheese

for the paneer skewers
75g fresh mint, finely chopped
4 tablespoons natural yogurt
50g finely grated mild cheddar
  cheese
2cm piece of root ginger, peeled and
  finely grated
2 garlic cloves, crushed
½ teaspoon cumin seeds, toasted
½ teaspoon marjoram, toasted
2 x 375g blocks paneer cheese
little sunflower oil for cooking
salt and freshly ground black pepper
large wooden bamboo skewers,
  soaked for 24 hours

6 tablespoons sunflower oil
juice of 2 lemons
2 tablespoons water
1 red onion, cut into thin rings
2 red peppers, deseeded and
  chopped
350g firm but ripe tomatoes,
  chopped
2 naan bread, cut or torn into pieces
1 red chilli, finely chopped
1cm piece of root ginger, peeled and
  finely grated
50g fresh coriander, roughly torn
25g fresh mint, roughly torn
salt and freshly ground black pepper

Mix together the mint, yogurt, grated cheddar and ginger in a bowl. Add the garlic, cumin, marjoram and a little seasoning to form a thick paste.

Cut the paneer into 8 x 5cm blocks, and then with a sharp small knife, cut down to divide each cheese into three sections, *without* cutting right through the base, about 1cm from the bottom. Using a small palette knife, smear the insides of all the cheeses thickly with the paste, then skewer two blocks lengthways with a soaked skewer (or two) to secure them while cooking.

Combine the oil, lemon juice and 2 tablespoons of water in a large bowl. Add the vegetables and toss well. Add the naan bread, chilli, ginger and herbs and mix well. Allow to stand for about 15 minutes for the flavours to meld. Season to taste.

Heat a ridged grill pan with a little oil. When hot, place the paneer skewers on it and grill for 3–4 minutes, turning them regularly, until lightly charred all over. Share the salad between four serving plates or bowls. Remove the cheese from the grill, arrange on the salad and serve immediately.

forever
summer

Fresh Cornish crab has an incomparable flavour. This salad makes a good first course for an early summer meal.

cornish crab & asparagus salad

with lemon vinaigarette

12 asparagus spears,
  peeled and well trimmed
1 head of red chicory (endive)
1 head of yellow chicory
2 avocados, peeled, stoned & sliced
2 carrots, cut into matchsticks
300g fresh white crabmeat
Parmesan shavings, to garnish
salt and freshly ground black pepper

for the vinaigrette
1 tablespoon Dijon mustard
1 small egg yolk
1 tablespoon lemon juice
finely grated zest of ¼ lemon
1 tablespoon champagne vinegar
  or white wine vinegar
5 tablespoons extra virgin olive oil
1½ tablespoons freshly grated
  Parmesan

Cook the asparagus spears in boiling salted water for 3–4 minutes until just tender. Drain and refresh in cold water, then dry thoroughly and cut lengthways in half.

For the dressing, whisk together the mustard, egg yolk, lemon juice and zest and vinegar, then whisk in the olive oil. Add the grated Parmesan cheese and season to taste.

Pull the leaves from the chicory, wash and dry them and arrange in alternating colours in a salad bowl or on serving plates. Put the asparagus, avocado, carrots and crabmeat in a separate bowl and toss gently with the dressing, then adjust the seasoning to taste. Scatter this mixture over the chicory leaves, sprinkle some coarsely cracked black pepper over the top (see PG TIPS on page 16) and then scatter liberally with the Parmesan shavings. Serve immediately.

middle-eastern beetroot & coriander salad

400g new season baby beetroot
200g red cherry tomatoes, halved
100g yellow cherry tomatoes, halved
juice of ½ lemon
6 tablespoons virgin olive oil
½ teaspoon coriander seeds, lightly
  cracked in a pestle and mortar
salt
Cayenne pepper
100g fresh coriander,
  leaves only
20 small balls of labna cheese
  (see PG TIPS)

Place the beetroot in a pan, cover with cold water and bring to the boil. Reduce the heat to a simmer and cook until they are just tender (alternatively, you could steam them). Drain well and peel. Cut the beetroot into halves or quarters, so they are approximately the same size as the tomatoes.

Put the beetroot and tomatoes in a large bowl and add the lemon juice, olive oil and coriander seeds. Season with salt and a little Cayenne and toss the whole lot together. Finally toss in the fresh coriander leaves, then serve, topped with the balls of labna cheese.

PG TIPS

Labna is a strained yogurt cheese, available from Middle Eastern food shops and some supermarkets. It is easy to make at home: simply strain some thick, Greek-style yogurt through a piece of muslin over a period of two days to drain off the whey, leaving you with a firm yogurt cheese. Roll into small balls between your hands.

Since the early days of *nouvelle cuisine*, when the Troisgros brothers created the spinach salad, many chefs have come up with variations on the theme. Here's mine. The spinach is tossed in a creamy goat's cheese dressing and topped with crisp *prosciutto*.

spinach salad

with crisp *prosciutto* and goat's cheese dressing

for the dressing:
75g mild goat's cheese
1 tablespoon sherry vinegar
3 tablespoons single cream
100ml olive oil
1 teaspoon Dijon mustard
1 teaspoon fresh thyme leaves
salt and freshly ground black pepper

8 thin slices of *prosciutto*, about
    120g in total
300g young spinach leaves
75g button mushrooms,
    thinly sliced
2 free-range eggs, hard-boiled and
    roughly chopped

For the dressing, blitz together the goat's cheese, vinegar, cream, olive oil, mustard and thyme in a blender or food processor until light and creamy. Season to taste with salt and plenty of black pepper.

Place the prosciutto slices under a hot grill until crisp on one side, then turn them over and grill until crisp on the other side. Drain on kitchen paper.

Put the spinach, mushrooms and chopped hard-boiled eggs in a bowl and gently toss with the dressing. Top with the grilled *prosciutto*.

PG TIPS
Although my recipe uses a mild goat's cheese, I have successfully replaced it with mascarpone cheese, which works equally well.

This delicate marinade adds a sweet yet hot coating to the tofu, topping a wonderfully fragrant and fresh salad.

red tofu salad

with beans, mint and cashews

250g pack firm tofu, drained
2 tablespoons plum sauce
2 tablespoons dark soy sauce
1 tablespoon honey
3 teaspoons sweet chilli sauce
325g French beans, topped and tailed
2 tablespoons cashew nuts, roasted
    and roughly chopped
2 persimmons (Sharon fruit), stems
    removed and cut into wedges
2 tablespoons groundnut or
    vegetable oil
salt and freshly ground black pepper

for the dressing
2 tablespoons palm sugar
    (or brown sugar)
2 tablespoons coarse sea salt
2 garlic cloves, chopped
good handful of mint leaves
4 hot green chillies, deseeded
    and chopped
1cm piece of root ginger, peeled
    and grated
3 tablespoons *nuoc mam chay*
    (vegetarian fish sauce) or *nam pla*
    (Thai fish sauce)
juice of 8 limes
4 shallots, thinly sliced
salt and freshly ground black pepper

Cut the tofu in half widthways, then cut both pieces in half horizontally to give four equally thick slices. In a shallow dish combine the plum sauce, soy sauce, honey and sweet chilli sauce. Place the tofu slices in the marinade and leave to marinate for 2 hours, turning them regularly to ensure the tofu is thoroughly coated. Cook the beans in a pan of boiling salted water for 2–3 minutes or until just cooked, but still retaining a good bite.

For the dressing, melt the palm sugar in a small pan. Place the salt, garlic and mint in a mortar and lightly pound to a pulp with a pestle. Add the chillies, palm sugar and ginger and pound again. Add the fish sauce, lime juice and shallots and mix well. Leave for 1 hour for the flavours to develop. Place the cashews, persimmons and beans in a bowl and pour over the prepared dressing. Toss well and season to taste.

Remove the tofu from the marinade. Heat a large frying pan with the oil, add the tofu and cook for about 2 minutes on each side until golden and crisp. Place a good pile of the salad on four serving plates, top each with 1–2 slices of tofu and serve at once.

slow-roasted tomato salad

with Tunisian hot dressing

12 firm, small to medium
  plum tomatoes, halved
½ teaspoon each of cumin and
  coriander seeds, roasted in a
  dry frying pan
1½ teaspoons coarse sea salt
2 teaspoons sugar
100ml olive oil

for the dressing:
1 teaspoon *harissa* paste
½ garlic clove, crushed
½ red onion, finely chopped
2 tablespoons chopped coriander
juice and zest of 1 orange
4 tablespoons groundnut oil

Preheat the oven to 110°C/225°F/gas mark ¼.

Place the tomatoes in a shallow baking tin, sprinkle over the roasted cumin and coriander seeds, sea salt, sugar and oil and roast slowly in the oven for about 25–30 minutes, until they begin to soften and dry slightly.

Meanwhile, combine all the ingredients for the dressing in a bowl and leave to stand at room temperature for the flavours to meld.

Put the warm tomatoes in a serving dish, pour over the spicy dressing and serve, either at room temperature or cold.

PG TIPS
Harissa is a North African hot red sauce made from chilli peppers, often smoked or dried. In Tunisia it is served with almost every meal. Rose *harissa,* which includes rose petals, is hard to find, but well worth the effort.

This fragrant Moroccan-style salad is highly spiced with *ras el hanout*, a North African spice mix. *Ras el hanout* is made up of some 30 different spices, including dried roses, cardamom, turmeric and cloves. Look for it in Middle Eastern shops and some specialist food shops. Serve this salad as a refreshing side dish.

date & blood orange salad

juice of 1 lime and 2 lemons
grated zest of ½ lime and 1 lemon
about ¾ teaspoon ground cinnamon
1 teaspoon orange flower water
2 tablespoons castor sugar
4 blood oranges, peeled
  and thickly sliced
12 fresh dates, halved, stoned
  and cut into strips
a pinch of *ras el hanout*

Put the lime and lemon juice and zest in a bowl, add a pinch of the cinnamon, plus the orange flower water and sugar and mix well. Leave for 1 hour at room temperature. Place in a pan and boil for 5 minutes to form a light syrup. Remove from the heat and leave to cool, then chill.

Place the orange slices and dates in a bowl and pour over the chilled syrup. Sprinkle over the *ras el hanout*, sprinkle over the remaining cinnamon to taste, and serve.

What constitutes a real Cæsar salad has long been a real bone of contention. How is the egg dressing made? Does it or doesn't it include anchovies? It really does come down to your preferred recipe, so here's mine.

cæsar salad

for the dressing
1 large free-range egg
1 teaspoon Worcester sauce
juice of half a lemon
1 garlic clove, crushed
4 salted anchovies, rinsed, dried, finely chopped
1 teaspoon superfine capers, rinsed, chopped
1 teaspoon Dijon mustard
freshly ground black pepper
75ml virgin olive oil
40g grated Parmesan cheese

for the salad
2 large crisp cos lettuces
50g plain toasted croûtons (made from a farmhouse style white loaf, cut into small dice and toasted in the oven)
extra Parmesan shavings, to scatter

For the dressing, immerse the egg in boiling water for one minute, remove and cool. Mix Worcester sauce, lemon juice, garlic, anchovies, capers and mustard in a bowl and add pepper. Crack the egg into the bowl and whisk until smooth. Slowly trickle in the oil in a steady stream, whisking until smooth and emulsified. Stir in the grated Parmesan.

Tear the cos lettuce leaves into roughly 2.5cm lengths, wash well and dry thoroughly. Place in a large bowl. Toss the leaves gently with the prepared dressing. Season to taste and arrange on a serving dish. Scatter over the toasted croûtons, extra Parmesan and serve.

PG TIPS
One of the recent innovations from America's Californian hotspots is the chicken Caesar salad, which is simply a grilled marinated breast of chicken, added hot off the grill on to the salad. This forms a nice light main dish, simple to prepare and quickly devoured.

This stunning ruby-coloured salad is one of my favourite summertime preparations – a combination of sweet and peppery flavours. I always prefer to cook my own beetroot at any time, although it's fine to use the cooked varieties sold packed in stores and supermarkets. However, be sure not to buy the pickled variety.

summer
ruby salad

for the dressing
4 tablespoons raspberry
  or red wine vinegar
½ teaspoon Dijon mustard
1 teaspoon maple syrup
6 tablespoons mild olive oil
salt and freshly ground black pepper

2 large cooked beetroots
  peeled and cut into 1cm dice
1 red onion, thinly sliced
8 red radishes
300g watermelon, cut into 1cm dice
100g red cabbage, very thinly sliced
20 fresh purple basil leaves
40g edible purple flowers
  (borage, lavender, pansies etc.)
salt and freshly ground black pepper

For the dressing, whisk together all the ingredients in a bowl and season to taste.

Place all the salad ingredients in another bowl, pour over the dressing, season to taste and toss together gently. Arrange the salad attractively on 4 serving plates and serve immediately.

PG TIPS
Diced buffalo mozzarella or goat's cheese makes a good addition to this salad. I also serve the salad dressed in a horseradish crème fraîche dressing, made by whisking together 1 tablespoon of sherry vinegar with 1 tablespoon of creamed horseradish, 100ml olive oil, 3 tablespoons of crème fraîche and seasoning.

For me, the combination of spinach and blue cheese is a spectacular one. Any type of blue cheese is suitable for this wonderfully fresh-tasting salad, scattered with nutritious pumpkin seeds. Just use your favourite.

spinach, blue cheese & avocado salad

with pumpkin seeds

350g tender young spinach leaves
100g mushrooms, washed and sliced
2 hard-boiled eggs, chopped
75g blue cheese, in 1cm cubes
1 garlic clove, crushed
200g fromage frais
1 teaspoon mild Dijon mustard
1 teaspoon lemon juice
salt and freshly ground black pepper
1 avocado, peeled, stoned and
   cut into 1cm cubes
12 slices of small baguette, toasted
50g pumpkin seeds, toasted

Put the spinach in a salad bowl and add the mushrooms, hard-boiled eggs and blue cheese. Mix together the garlic, fromage frais, mustard and lemon juice to make a dressing and toss carefully with the salad. Season to taste.

Arrange on serving plates, top with the avocado and toasted baguette slices and sprinkle over the toasted pumpkin seeds. Serve immediately.

PG TIPS
Other vegetables, such as leeks, artichokes and even asparagus, can be cooked and then prepared in the same way for this salad. Pumpkin seeds are quite easy to find in health shops, but sunflower seeds make a tasty alternative if necessary.

A simple and delicious salad containing lots of texture and flavour – the curry powder gives the vegetables an added zing. Easy to prepare; a real winner!

chickpea salad

with beetroot, cauliflower and curried egg dressing

12 baby beetroot with stems, washed
100ml water
1 small cauliflower, separated
   into small florets
4 cos lettuce leaves
75g rocket leaves
400g tinned chickpeas, drained
   and rinsed
50g freshly picked coriander leaves

for the dressing
½ garlic clove, flattened with the
   back of a knife
1 teaspoon Dijon mustard
1 teaspoon mild curry powder
65ml mayonnaise
juice of ½ lemon
4 tablespoons water
1 tablespoon crème fraîche
2 eggs, hard-boiled and chopped
freshly ground black pepper

Preheat the oven to 200°C/400°F/gas mark 6.

Place the beetroots in a pouch of foil with the water and scrunch up the foil to secure the beetroots within. Place in the oven for 40 minutes, or until tender when pierced with a small knife. Remove and leave to cool. When cool enough to handle, peel them.

Cook the cauliflower florets in boiling water until just tender, but firm. Refresh in cold water and drain well.

To make the dressing, rub the inside of a bowl with the garlic clove, and then discard it. Put in the mustard, curry powder and mayonnaise and mix well. Then add the lemon juice, water, the crème fraîche and chopped egg and season with black pepper to taste. The dressing should be thick, but still pourable.

Place all the leaves in a large bowl, add the beetroots, cauliflower and chickpeas and a little of the dressing. Serve on 4 plates, coating the cauliflower with a little more dressing and scattering over the coriander leaves.

Vietnamese coriander can be found in Asian stores, although regular coriander could be substituted.

grilled baby aubergine salad

with roasted rice and coriander dressing

4 tablespoons sunflower oil
8 baby aubergines

for the dressing
zest of 1 lime
juice of 4 limes
1 tablespoon palm sugar
  (or brown sugar)
1 small green chilli
2 teaspoons *ketjap manis*
  (Indonesian soy sauce) or soy
  sauce
2 teaspoons dry-roasted basmati rice
  (see PG TIPS)
2 banana shallots, peeled and
  thinly sliced (or use normal
  shallots)
100g fresh Vietnamese
  coriander leaves (or coriander)
50g fresh mint leaves
salt and freshly ground black pepper

Heat a ridged grill pan over a high heat and brush with the oil. Cut the aubergines in half lengthways, place on the grill and cook for about 6–8 minutes, turning them regularly, until golden and lightly charred all over.

For the dressing, place the zest and juice of the limes, the palm sugar, chilli and soy sauce in a bowl and stir until the sugar has dissolved. Add the roasted rice, sliced shallots, coriander and mint leaves, season to taste and mix well.

Place the grilled aubergines on a large serving platter, spoon over the dressing and serve immediately.

PG TIPS

To prepare Asian-style roasted rice, heat the oven to 180°C/350°F/gas mark 4. Place 10g basmati rice in a baking tray and put in the oven to dry-roast for 20–25 minutes until golden. Remove and cool. Place in a mortar and crush with the pestle to a coarse powder. Keep in a sealed jar ready for use.

A wonderful crisp summer salad. Be sure to use prime quality vegetables and serve them warm, which really brings out the flavour.

summer
vegetable salad

300g asparagus, trimmed
300g baby carrots, trimmed
8 baby courgettes, trimmed
200g sugarsnap peas,
   trimmed
200g baby leeks, trimmed
2 tablespoons white wine vinegar
4 organic or free-range eggs
2 tablespoons pine kernels,
   toasted

for the dressing
3 tablespoons balsamic vinegar
salt and freshly ground black pepper
4 tablespoons extra virgin olive oil
4 tablespoons chopped basil
   (a mixture of purple and
   green looks good)

Bring a large pan of salted water to the boil, add the asparagus and simmer for 3–4 minutes, until tender. Remove with a slotted spoon and place in a large bowl of iced water (this helps preserve the colour). Drain immediately and set aside.

Return the water to the boil and cook the other vegetables in it until just tender, then plunge them into iced waters. When all the vegetables are cooked, mix them together in a large bowl and set aside.

For the dressing, put the balsamic vinegar in a bowl, add some salt and pepper, then beat in the olive oil and basil. Set aside.

Bring a large pan of water to the boil, add the white wine vinegar, then reduce the heat and poach the eggs in it. Meanwhile, warm the vegetables in a little boiling water for 1 minute, or place in a microwave for 30 seconds. Arrange the drained vegetables on 4 serving plates, spoon over the basil dressing and sprinkle over the pine kernels. Place a poached egg on the side of each salad and serve immediately.

salad of palm hearts, beetroot & asparagus

with pomegranate dressing

2 medium-sized beetroots
2 tablespoons olive oil
16 asparagus tips, trimmed
4 palm hearts (tinned), sliced
  lengthways
2 red chicory, leaves separated
100g watercress, stems removed
10 fresh basil leaves
2 tablespoons pistachio nuts,
  roughly chopped

for the pomegranate dressing
150ml fresh orange juice
1 tablespoon fresh lemon juice
1 tablespoon white wine vinegar
2 tablespoons mild olive oil
1 tablespoon vegetable oil
1 fresh pomegranate
salt and freshly ground black pepper

Preheat the oven to 180°C/350°F/gas mark 4. Wash the beetroots, drizzle with olive oil and wrap them in tinfoil. Place on a baking tray and bake in the oven for 1 hour or until just tender. Remove and cool slightly before peeling and then cut each one into ten wedges. Cook the asparagus in boiling salted water for 1 minute, drain and then refresh in cold water.

For the dressing, place the orange and lemon juice in a small pan and cook over a moderate heat until the liquid has reduced by half and become slightly syrupy. Pour into a bowl and leave to cool. Stir in the vinegar and whisk in both oils. Cut the pomegranate in half horizontally and then squeeze out the fruit in the palm of your hand to release the inner seeds, removing any bitter yellow membrane. Add the seeds and the juice to the dressing and season to taste.

Place all the salad ingredients in a bowl, pour over the dressing and toss lightly together. Place on 4 serving plates, drizzle over any excess dressing and serve.

Quinoa (pronounced 'keen-wah'), has a nutty flavour, and is high in protein and iron. It needs to be well rinsed, then lightly toasted prior to cooking in water or a stock. It is fast becoming a trendy grain, loved by vegetarians and meat-eaters alike. I often serve this salad along with some *hummus*, pitta bread and tossed greens.

quinoa & feta tabbouleh

200g quinoa
500ml water
200g, cherry tomatoes, halved
100g seeded cucumber
  cut into 1cm cubes
1 onion, finely chopped
3 tablespoons chopped
  flat leaf parsley
1 tablespoon chopped
  fresh mint leaves
1 tablespoon chopped
  fresh coriander
150g crumbled feta cheese
50g pitted black olives
juice of 1 large lemon
4 tablespoons olive oil
salt and freshly ground black pepper

Place the quinoa in a bowl, cover with warm water and rub between your hands: the water will turn cloudy. Repeat several times until the water remains clear. Drain well.

Heat a large, dry non-stick frying pan over medium heat, add quinoa and toast until golden, stirring constantly.

Bring 500ml water to the boil in a saucepan, add the toasted quinoa, reduce the heat, and simmer for about 12 minutes until tender, but not mushy. Drain and rinse with cold water. Drain well.

In a large bowl toss the quinoa with the remaining ingredients and season to taste. Leave to stand for 20 minutes before serving.

The combination of smoked fish and fruit is legendary, as the fruit not only counteracts the richness of the fish, but also gives a pleasant freshness to the salad.

smoked trout, orange & blueberry salad

with rocket and tarragon dressing

6 sweet navel oranges
2 tablespoons castor sugar
2 teaspoons Dijon mustard
2 teaspoons arrowroot, dissolved in
    65ml cold water
2 tablespoons chopped tarragon
250g blueberries
2 tablespoons pine kernels, toasted
300g rocket leaves
400g smoked trout, skin removed
    and flaked

Squeeze the juice from 2 of the oranges. Place in a non-stick pan, add the sugar and mustard and bring to the boil. Whisk in the dissolved arrowroot, reduce the heat and stir until thickened. Allow to cool.

Using a small knife, peel the remaining oranges, ensuring all the white pith is removed. Cut the oranges into quarters lengthways, then cut crossways to form thick slices.

Place in a bowl, add the orange and arrowroot mixture, tarragon, blueberries, pine kernels and rocket leaves and toss to coat. Sprinkle over the flaked smoked trout and serve.

winter warmers

I have always liked the combination of smoked fish and potatoes. Here, Jersey Royals and a piquant dressing act as the perfect foil for the salmon.

roast
potato salad

with smoked salmon

350g small Jersey Royal potatoes
150ml olive oil
salt and freshly ground black pepper
2 tablespoons sherry vinegar
2 spring onions, cut into 3mm slices
1 tablespoon superfine
  capers, drained
6 small cocktail gherkins,
  thinly sliced
2 eggs, hard-boiled and
  finely chopped
300g thinly sliced smoked salmon
1 teaspoon chopped tarragon

Preheat the oven to 190°C/375°F/gas mark 5. Wash the potatoes, then put them in a roasting tin, toss with 60ml of the olive oil, and season with salt. Roast for about 40 minutes, until golden and tender, then remove from the oven and leave to cool slightly.

Whisk the vinegar and the remaining olive oil together to make a dressing and season to taste. Cut the potatoes in half and place in a bowl with the spring onions, capers, gherkins and chopped eggs. Pour over the dressing and adjust the seasoning.

Spread the smoked salmon out on 4 serving plates and arrange the potato salad on top. If you're a salmon lover like me, place a little extra salmon on top, too. Sprinkle with the tarragon and serve.

I love the smoky flavours that predominate in this salad. The tart vinaigrette makes an ideal dressing for the charred leeks. If possible, cook the vegetables on a barbecue.

leek, red onion & smoked mozzarella salad

a pinch of sugar
salt
24 young leeks, trimmed
2 red onions, cut into wedges
freshly ground black pepper
1 smoked mozzarella cheese,
   (or use natural mozzarella)
   cut into 8 thin slices

for the vinaigrette
3 tablespoons tarragon vinegar
   or champagne vinegar
1 teaspoon Dijon mustard
1 tablespoon chopped fresh tarragon
135ml extra virgin olive oil
1 tomato, deseeded and finely diced
1 tablespoon superfine
   capers, rinsed and drained
1 tablespoon green olives, stoned
   and finely chopped
1 hard-boiled egg, chopped

Bring a large pan of water to the boil with the sugar and a little salt. Throw in the leeks, return to the boil and cook gently for 2–3 minutes. Drain them well and dry on a cloth.

For the vinaigrette, mix the vinegar, mustard and tarragon together in a bowl and then whisk in the olive oil. Add all the remaining ingredients and season to taste with salt and pepper.

Grill the leeks and onions – for the best flavour this should be done on a barbecue or a ridged cast-iron grill pan, but you can also cook them under a preheated grill. When they are tender and slightly blackened, remove from the heat and season with salt and pepper.

Toss the leeks and onions with the vinaigrette and adjust the seasoning. Arrange on serving plates, drape 2 slices of mozzarella over each portion and serve.

Pumpkins flood the shops in late autumn, and can easily be turned into this warming treat. At other times of year, this colourful Asian-influenced salad works equally well using butternut squash.

spice-grilled pumpkin salad

1 garlic clove, crushed
1 teaspoon ground cumin
2 red chillies, finely chopped
4 tablespoons rice wine vinegar
1 tablespoon soft brown sugar
2 tablespoons *ketjap manis* (Indonesian soy sauce) or soy sauce
3 tablespoons olive oil
1 tablespoon dark sesame oil
1 small pumpkin (or butternut squash), deseeded and cut into wedges
2 tablespoons chopped coriander (optional)

Place the garlic, cumin, chillies, vinegar and sugar in a saucepan, bring to the boil, then reduce the heat and simmer until the mixture has reduced to a light syrup. Transfer to a large bowl and add the soy sauce, olive oil and sesame oil.

Cook the pumpkin wedges in boiling salted water for 10 minutes, then drain well and place in the chilli oil. Leave to marinate for 1 hour.

Heat a ridged grill pan, place the pumpkin pieces on it and cook for 10–12 minutes, until caramelised, turning regularly. Serve the salad warm, sprinkled with the coriander, if liked.

warm
steak salad

with horseradish, mustard and balsamic juices

for the dressing
1 teaspoon Dijon mustard
1 teaspoon grated horseradish root
1 garlic clove, crushed
4 tablespoons balsamic vinegar
125ml vegetable oil
salt and freshly ground black pepper
1 tablespoon chopped coriander
100ml meat stock

2 tablespoons vegetable oil
450g best quality beef fillet
salt and freshly ground black pepper
150g bag of mixed salad leaves
1 large carrot, cut into 3mm strips
½ celeriac, cut into 3mm strips
1 large beetroot, cut into 3mm strips
1 red onion, thinly sliced

For the dressing, place the mustard, horseradish and garlic in a bowl, add the vinegar and leave for 10–15 minutes to infuse. Whisk in the oil to form a dressing. Season with salt and pepper and add the coriander.

Heat the vegetable oil in a small frying pan until almost smoking. Season the beef fillet with salt and pepper, add to the pan and fry over a moderate heat for 8–10 minutes, turning once (alternatively cook in a hot oven for 5–8 minutes); this should give medium-rare to medium meat. Remove from the pan and keep warm.

Return the pan in which the meat was cooked to the heat and add the meat stock. Bring to the boil and boil for 1 minute, stirring and scraping the bottom of the pan to deglaze, then add the liquid to the dressing and mix thoroughly.

Place the salad leaves, vegetable strips and onion slices in a bowl and toss with half the dressing. Place the salad on 4 serving plates. Slice the beef thinly and arrange on top of the salad. Pour on the remaining dressing and serve.

This salad is a joy – it uses the first of the new season Jersey Royal potatoes. However, potato farmers often dig these from the ground too early these days, which is a great shame.

baby beet, potato & blue cheese salad

6 baby beetroots, whole
   or cut in half, depending on size
3 tablespoons olive oil
1 tablespoon good quality
   red wine vinegar
1 heaped teaspoon brown sugar
450g baby Jersey Royal potatoes
175g Stilton or gorgonzola
   cheese, roughly chopped
3 tablespoons walnut oil
3 tablespoons walnut halves,
   toasted and roughly chopped
coarse salt and freshly cracked
   black pepper
juice of 1 lemon

Preheat the oven to 200°C/400°F/gas mark 6. Trim the beetroots and wash them well. Place in a roasting tin, drizzle with the olive oil and red wine vinegar, then sprinkle with the brown sugar. Roast in the oven for 40–45 minutes, until tender.

Cook the potatoes in their skins in boiling salted water until tender, then drain well and cut in half. Put them in a bowl with the cooked beetroot and scatter the cheese on top. Drizzle over the walnut oil, scatter over the walnuts, then season with coarse salt and cracked black pepper.

roquefort & red cabbage salad

with roasted walnut vinaigrette

¼ red cabbage, central core removed,
   thinly sliced
4 tablespoons red wine vinegar
50g castor sugar
600ml water
100g streaky bacon, cut into 2cm dice
2 slices of white bread, cut into
   1cm cubes
1 garlic clove, crushed
2 heads of chicory (endive)
1 small head of radicchio
150g Roquefort (or any blue cheese),
   crumbled

for the vinaigrette
4 tablespoons red wine vinegar
1 teaspoon Dijon mustard
4 tablespoons walnut oil
4 tablespoons olive oil
2 tablespoons walnuts, roasted
   and broken into chunks
salt and freshly ground black pepper

Put the cabbage in a bowl. Bring the vinegar to the boil, add the sugar and, once dissolved, pour it over the cabbage and stir well. Boil the water and pour that over the cabbage too. Leave to soak for 5 minutes, then drain in a colander and leave to cool.

Heat a frying pan over a high heat, add the bacon and cook until it is crisp and the fat has been released. Add the bread and fry until golden, then stir in the garlic and fry for 1 minute. Remove from the heat. Put the red cabbage in a salad bowl with the chicory and radicchio leaves, scatter over the bacon and croûtons and the Roquefort cheese.

Whisk together all the ingredients for the vinaigrette and pour it over the salad. Toss well, adjust the seasoning and serve.

PG TIPS

To roast nuts, toss them in a little oil, season lightly, then place on a baking sheet and bake in an oven preheated to 180°C/350°F/gas mark 4 for 5–8 minutes, or until toasted in flavour and colour. Cool before use. I have on occasion replaced the red cabbage with finely shredded beetroot.

Lamb and mint form a combination that everyone is familiar with. I took it a stage further to create this wonderful salad.

salad of grilled lamb fillet

with blue cheese & warm mint dressing

4 lamb fillets, about 75g each
100g French beans
8–12 thin slices cut from a small
   baguette
olive oil, for brushing
a handful each of frisée and
   spinach leaves
2 tomatoes, skinned, deseeded
   and cut into strips
65g button mushrooms, thinly
   sliced
50g hard blue cheese, diced
   (Stilton, blue Wensleydale, or my
   favourite, Lanark Blue)

for the dressing
4 tablespoons double cream
1 tablespoon clear honey
50g hard blue cheese, crumbled
1 tablespoon sherry vinegar
2 tablespoons olive oil
1 tablespoon chopped fresh mint
2 tablespoons hot water
salt and freshly ground
   black pepper

Season the lamb fillets and cook on a ridged cast-iron grill pan (or under a hot grill or in a frying pan) for 5–8 minutes, until done but still rosy inside. Keep warm.

Meanwhile, cook the French beans in boiling salted water until just tender, then drain and refresh in cold water. Drain again and dry.

For the dressing, put the cream and honey in a pan and bring to the boil, then remove from the heat. Add the cheese and allow it to melt into the cream. Whisk in the vinegar, olive oil and mint, then whisk in the water and season to taste.

Brush the slices of bread with olive oil and grill on both sides until they are lightly browned. Put the frisée and spinach leaves in a bowl, add the tomatoes, French beans, mushrooms and cheese, then toss with the warm dressing. Put in the centre of 4 serving plates. Slice the grilled lamb fillets and arrange around the salad. Top the salad with the croûtons and serve immediately.

A sexy potato salad with colours to set the tastebuds dancing in anticipation. Purple truffle potatoes (sometimes sold as black potatoes) are becoming increasingly available now but any variety of firm, waxy potato could be used instead.

truffle potato salad

with warm pesto dressing

450g truffle potatoes

for the dressing
100ml virgin olive oil
2 garlic cloves, peeled
2 tablespoons pine kernels
75g fresh basil leaves
2 tablespoons freshly grated
  Parmesan cheese
a pinch of sugar
salt and freshly ground black pepper

Steam or boil the potatoes in their skins until just tender, about 15–20 minutes. Drain well and leave until cool enough to handle.

Meanwhile for the dressing, warm the olive oil in a saucepan with the garlic for 2–3 minutes to infuse the oil, then add the pine kernels and basil and leave over a low heat for a further 2–3 minutes. Place in a blender and blitz until smooth. Mix in the Parmesan and season with the sugar, salt and freshly ground black pepper.

Peel the potatoes and place in a warm salad bowl. Pour the warm pesto dressing over the potatoes and serve immediately.

Serving sweet-tasting beetroot with hot piquant horseradish has always been a marriage made in heaven. The addition of the basil adds a touch of elegance. I often serve this as part of a buffet.

roasted beetroot & basil salad

with creamed horseradish dressing

24 baby beetroot
10 basil leaves, snipped into
   small pieces

for the dressing
6 tablespoons soured cream
   or crème fraîche
2 tablespoons grated horseradish root
2 tablespoons cider vinegar
2 teaspoons Dijon mustard
½ teaspoon grated lemon zest
salt and freshly ground black pepper
6 tablespoons vegetable oil

Preheat the oven to 180°C/350°F/gas mark 4. Trim the beetroot tops, leaving 2cm of the stalk attached. Wash them well, then wrap them in 2 foil packages, place on a baking sheet and roast for 1–1½ hours or until tender.

Unwrap the beetroot and leave until cool enough to handle. Peel them, cut in half and place in a large bowl.

For the dressing, whisk together the soured cream or crème fraîche, horseradish, vinegar, mustard, lemon zest and some seasoning. Add the oil in a thin stream, whisking until emulsified.

Pour the dressing over the beetroot, toss well together and transfer to a salad bowl. Scatter over the basil and serve.

The dark greeny-blue French *lentilles du Puy* are generally considered to have the best flavour and are well worth buying. Cannellini beans also work very well in this winter salad.

warm lentil salad

with grilled goat's cheese & anchovy toasts

200g Puy lentils
1 onion, finely chopped
1 teaspoon cumin seeds
4 tablespoons olive oil
2 tablespoons balsamic vinegar or
  white wine vinegar
1 shallot, finely chopped

for the toasts
6 canned anchovy fillets,
  rinsed and dried
1 egg yolk
5 tablespoons olive oil
4 slices of French bread,
  cut 1.5cm thick
4 Capricorn goat's cheeses,
  cut horizontally in half
1 tablespoon fresh thyme or
  rosemary leaves
1 tablespoon coarsely ground
  black peppercorns

Put the lentils in a saucepan, cover with cold water and bring to the boil, skimming off any impurities that rise to the surface. Add the onion and cumin seeds and simmer for 30–40 minutes, until the lentils are just tender. Drain them well. Mix the olive oil, vinegar and shallot together and stir into the lentils. Keep warm.

For the cheese and anchovy toasts, work the anchovies and egg yolk to a paste with a pestle and mortar, then gradually blend in the olive oil to give a thick purée. Toast the French bread and spread with the anchovy paste, then top each one with 2 pieces of goat's cheese. Sprinkle over the thyme or rosemary leaves and black pepper and place under a hot grill until lightly browned. Put the warm lentils on serving plates, top with the toasts and serve straight away.

PG TIPS
Because the quantities for the anchovy paste are small, you really need to use a pestle and mortar. However, if you double the amount, you can blitz everything together in a blender. You are bound to find a use for the surplus; store it in the fridge and toss with pasta or use in sandwiches.

Salsas and *mojos* are an important element of Latin American cooking. They typically contain garlic, a citrus juice and herbs. *Mojos* are more liquid than *salsas*, and are traditionally served with cooked foods, as in this piquant salad.

grilled vegetable salad

(*mojo criolla*)

for the dressing
2 garlic cloves, crushed
1 hot red chilli, deseeded
   and finely chopped
1 teaspoon cumin seeds, toasted
salt
100ml extra-virgin olive oil
50ml fresh orange juice
2 teaspoons sherry vinegar
1 teaspoon tomato ketchup
freshly ground black pepper

100ml olive oil
2 large red peppers, deseeded
   and cut into thick strips
2 large yellow peppers, deseeded
   and cut into thick strips
12 baby sweetcorn
6 small courgettes,
   halved lengthways
12 asparagus tips
9 baby leeks, trimmed
4 palm hearts (tinned), cut into
   long batons
1 tablespoon superfine capers
1 avocado, peeled, stoned and
   cut into 1cm dice

For the dressing, place the garlic, chilli, cumin seeds and a little salt in a mortar and crush with a pestle to a smooth paste. Heat the olive oil in a pan and, when hot, add the garlic paste. Remove from the heat and leave to stand for 5 minutes, before adding the orange juice, vinegar and tomato ketchup. Season to taste, leave to cool and refrigerate.

Heat a ridged grill pan until smoking. Drizzle in the olive oil and grill the peppers and baby sweetcorn for 5 minutes on each side or until the skins are blistered and charred. Transfer the peppers to a bowl, lightly cover with clingfilm and leave to steam for 20 minutes. Peel the peppers and place in a large bowl along with the baby sweetcorn.

Place the remaining vegetables on the grill pan and grill until cooked and lightly charred. Place all the vegetables in a bowl, then add a little dressing to the vegetables and toss gently together. Add the capers and diced avocado and toss again. Place in a huge pile, drizzle over the remaining dressing and serve at room temperature.

roquefort stuffed fig salad

with port vinaigrette and frozen avocado cream

for the avocado cream
150g sugar
65ml water
2 avocados (preferably Haas variety)
250ml dry white wine
juice of ½ lemon
4 tablespoons whipping cream

for the salad
8 large figs
120g Roquefort cheese
1 tablespoon honey
1 teaspoon truffle oil (optional)
olive oil
100g young rocket leaves
100g watercress, any tough stems
   removed
1 avocado, peeled, stoned and cut
   into small dice
50g spiced pecan nuts

for the port vinaigrette
2 tablespoons olive oil
1 shallot, finely chopped
100ml port
3 tablespoons balsamic vinegar
1 tablespoon honey
juice of ½ lemon
salt and freshly ground black pepper

For the avocado cream, place the sugar and water in a pan, bring to the boil and simmer for 1 minute to make a light syrup. Leave to cool. Peel and remove the stone from the avocados, cut the flesh into pieces and blend with the syrup, white wine and lemon juice until smooth. Add the cream, then transfer to an ice-cream machine. Freeze overnight.

Remove a third off the top of each fig and scoop out a little of the flesh. Mix together the cheese, scooped out flesh, honey and truffle oil, then stuff each fig with the mixture and replace the tops. Set aside.

For the vinaigrette, heat the olive oil in a pan, add the shallot and cook for 30 seconds. Add the port, vinegar, honey and lemon juice and boil for 1 minute. Season to taste, sieve to remove lumps, and keep warm.

Preheat the oven to 220°C/425°F/gas mark 7. Place the figs on a baking dish, drizzle over a little olive oil and bake in the oven for 5–6 minutes until just softened.

Toss the rocket and watercress with the avocado, spiced nuts and warm port dressing. Serve on plates with two stuffed figs and a scoop of avocado cream.

index

112